MW00885289

Connect with us!

We'd love to get in touch with you on social media! You can follow Real Live Faith on Facebook, Instagram, and Gab Social for daily Biblical encouragement, and keep up with new resources and publishing releases!

Follow us on Facebook @reallivefaith.co

Follow us on Instagram @reallivefaith.co

Follow us on Gab Social @RealLiveFaith

When you complete this devotional, share with us how one year of praying for your business has impacted you, your employees, and your company!

#reallivefaith

Table of Contents

MISSION

WHAT'S THE MISSION
OF YOUR COMPANY?

These next 6 weeks, pray and ask God to remind you of your mission as a company. And ask God to remind you of your purpose as a Christian entrepreneur. Ask Him to bring these to mind and to help you focus on Him and the plans He has for your business.

Dear Lord,

Help me to _____

_____
(insert the mission of your company)

And help me as I _____

_____
*(insert your purpose as a Christian
entrepreneur in the marketplace)*

I ask that You remind me
often of this mission and
purpose so I don't lose
sight of my calling.

AMEN

"So whether you eat or drink or *whatever you do,* do it all for the glory of God."

1 Corinthians 10:31

What do you do?
What is your business about?

Seek to "do it all for the glory of
God." What does that mean? The
purpose of our lives is to glorify
God – doing that which pleases
Him and brings Him honor.

Set a goal for yourself.
What's one way you can glorify
God in your business this week?

Copy this week's verse onto a
notecard and keep it nearby all
week. Meditate on the words and
commit the verse to memory.
Reflect on "whatever you do"
as a business and seek to
"do it all for the glory of God."

Dear LORD,

Help me to remember my mission and purpose. Help me to bring honor and glory to Your name in all I do, in all I say, in all I post, in all I record, and in all I make. I pray You be exalted over my work in all I do. Take away anything in my work that doesn't bring You honor and glory.

AMEN

Add to this prayer or write your own in the space provided. This is your time with the Lord to meditate on this week's verse and talk to Him about your business, bring Him on staff and involve Him in your company.

_____

_____

_____

_____

_____

_____

_____

_____

"Whatever you do, work at it with all your heart, as working for the Lord, not for human masters, since you know that you will receive an inheritance from the Lord as a reward. It is the Lord Christ you are serving."

Colossians 3:23-24

This week, specifically, pray and ask the Lord to remind you Who you work for.

Remember and reflect on the last part of verse 24, "It is the Lord Christ you are serving." How are you serving Him? We serve Him with our time, talents, and treasures.

Copy this week's verse onto a notecard and keep it nearby all week. Meditate on the words and commit the verse to memory. Reflect on doing your work "with all your heart" and work as you are "working for the Lord."

Dear LORD,

I pray You help me to do all I do with all my heart – 100% effort – as I work for You. Remind me, Lord, that ultimately my work is done out of love, faithfulness, and obedience to You. I thank You, Lord, that every good gift, blessing, and reward I receive on earth comes from You. Help me to not get weary in my work or lazy with the tasks I have each week. Help me to not produce low quality or inferior work. Help me to not be tempted to take short cuts in my work that may end up costing me in my character and integrity. Help me to not rush my work and risk producing less than You know I'm capable of. Give me Your strength and joy in my work each day.

AMEN

According to Colossians 3:23-24, Who do you ultimately work for? Who gives you your reward in the end?

_____

_____

_____

_____

_____

_____

"For we are God's handiwork, created in Christ Jesus to do good works, which God prepared in advance for us to do."

Ephesians 2:10

This week, pray and ask the Lord to remind you that you are His handiwork and that you were created to do good works that He prepared for you long ago.

We are God's masterpiece. His workmanship. He fashioned us and formed us and He is proud of His creation. Remember this week Who made you. Remember your Creator. You aren't just anybody. You are somebody special and unique to the One who made you. Spend some time this week giving praise and thanksgiving to God for the gifts, talents, and abilities He has given you. Seek Him for guidance in how you use those gifts and talents in your business. Be determined to use them to bring God glory and to draw others to the Lord.

Ephesians 2:10 encapsulates the purpose of our lives. We were created for the purpose of doing good works. Not just any works, but good works. And not just any good works, but the good works that God has prepared. It is He who has prepared the good works that we are to be doing. And they were not prepared on a whim or out of desperation or in haste. They were planned and prepared in advance (with purpose and intention) – just for us. This week, pray and ask the Lord to help you see those good works and to have open eyes that will be focused on those good works that He has prepared. Pray and ask Him to help you not to get distracted by the works the world tries to clutter your calendar with.

Dear LORD,

Thank You for showing me that I am Your handiwork, Your masterpiece, and workmanship. Thank You for fashioning me, forming me, and making me "custom made." Remind me of that truth when I am tempted to discount my worth and value as Your creation. Remind me of the truth found in Ephesians 2:10 when I am frustrated in my work or feeling weak in my abilities with my business. Help me to have eyes to see the good works You have created me for. And help me to complete them. Give me the strength, wisdom, and discernment needed. Help me to be obedient to what You have called me to do. And Lord, I pray these good works would bear fruit not only in my life and my business, but in others – ultimately leading them to salvation in You.

AMEN

Pray this week and ask God to help you know what the good works are. Ask Him to show them to you and point them out so you can do them. Ask Him for guidance and direction to carry them out in your life, family, and business.

_____

_____

_____

_____

_____

"The man who plants
and the man who
waters have one
purpose, and each will
be rewarded according
to his own labor. For
we are God's fellow
workers; you are God's
field, God's building."

1 Corinthians 3:8-9

"The man who plants" and "the man who waters." We are on the same team. We are both necessary. We both need each other. We are both working towards the same goal. We don't have to be jealous of the gifts, talents, or even the success of others because our reward is not given based on those. Our reward is given based on our own labor. God rewards us for the work we do, not for the results of the work – because the results belong to Him. Where do you need to let go of comparison in your work?

Notice how "one plants" and "one waters"...but it doesn't mention one who harvests, and that's because it's the Lord's job and not ours. We are not able to produce fruit in another person's life. All we can do is labor and God brings the increase. We can only do what He's called us to do ("labor") and whatever comes of it is His and it's for His glory. Therefore, we receive the reward for that which we have done, and we receive the reward whether or not anything comes of it, because we've been faithful to do what God called us to do. He rewards us for the work, not the results. Ask the Lord this week to show you the planting or the watering that needs done. Seek His help to not become envy of other workers.

"For we are God's fellow workers", which implies that we work alongside Him. What a humbling thing to be considered His fellow worker, His co-worker. How amazing! And it's only possible through Christ! We can't work without God. He is our working partner. He allows us to participate in His work. It's exciting and honorable to think that He would choose us to be part of His work. He doesn't have to do that. He is fully capable of doing His work all by Himself. Afterall, He made the world and all that is in it. This week, give thanks to God for allowing you this amazing opportunity to be His co-worker! Ask the Lord this week to help you focus on your own tasks and to complete them with a joyful and willing heart.

"...you are God's field, God's building." He is cultivating your life in order that you might bring forth fruit for His glory. You are the work of God.

Dear LORD,

Remind me that my job may be planting and another person's job may be watering. But together, we have one purpose and that is to glorify You and bring honor to Your name and share the Gospel. And remind me when I am overwhelmed or weary that I am rewarded for my own work – whether as a planter or a waterer. But together, we are fellow workers of You. Build unity in my company. Protect the company from the attacks of the enemy who try to divide us. Help us to have peace with one another in our work because we are Your field, Your building. Help me to build up Your building and not to tear it down.

AMEN

This week, pray and ask the Lord to remind you that you are His worker, His canvas and platform and tool with which His plans and purposes are fulfilled.

_____

_____

_____

_____

_____

_____

"Unless the Lord builds a house, They who build it labor in vain; Unless the Lord guards a city, The watchman stays awake in vain. It is futile for you to rise up early, To stay up late, To eat the bread of painful labor; This is how He gives to His beloved sleep."

Psalm 127:1-2

Spend some time this week in prayer asking the Lord to set your heart right with Him, and seek Him to build your business. We can't do it like He can and we don't know all that's needed like He does. We don't know the future. But He has already gone before us. Pray and seek His wisdom above the world's wisdom or your own wisdom. Ask Him to guide you and to show you what to do, when to do it, and how to do it. Ask Him to build your business and seek Him to use you wherever and however needed.

It's all about choosing the *right* builder. We can't do it on our own. We're not able. We need God! What's impossible for us, is possible for Him. God is our general contractor and we are His workers. All building design comes from Him.

Dear LORD,

Unless You bless the building, it is of no purpose for me to build. Without Your blessing, all is vain – all is nothing. Please, Lord, protect my business from enemy fire and enemy attacks. Lord, patrol the walls of my business. Help me, Lord, to not strive and hustle with the world, in eager pursuit of wealth. That's not from You. Thank You, Lord, for Your love and that You call us Your beloved. Help our minds to be at ease and our lives comfortably set on You – as our Master Builder and the Builder of all we are, and all we have, and all we do. Help us to be fervent students of Your Word more than anything else. Sleep and rest are a gift from You to us. And when we vainly strive after the world and pursue its wealth for ungodly gain, we will only fail, fall, be disappointed, and it will all be in vain because we left You out of everything. Help us, Lord, to want Your will and plan more than our own.

AMEN

This week, reflect on the fact that God is the One who builds. It all comes from His hand. We are just the stewards of what He so graciously gives to us. We can do no good or success unless He is at the center, and wholly involved in the process.

_____

_____

_____

"In everything,
therefore, treat
people the same
way you want
them to treat you,
for this is the Law
and the Prophets."

Matthew 7:12

As a business owner, there arc many opportunities to have contact with other people. So there are multiple opportunities to put this verse into practice – treating others as you would want to be treated. Consider the people you "treated" yesterday or last week. Were there any encounters you wish would've gone more smoothly? Did you feel like any of the encounters were a divine intervention? Or perhaps divine interruption? Take some time to reflect on those "meetings" and how the Lord may have used those opportunities to teach you about how we treat others, and how they treat us.

So often, we have more examples of how not to treat others. We have had bad encounters with internet providers, or supply chain issues, or cranky customers who were not very understanding of situations that were out of our control. Sometimes people are quick to give bad reviews more than they are willing to give a good review. And so we are tempted to "treat" them the same way they treat us. But our verse this week challenges us to do the opposite.

What a great verse this week to highlight what our focus has been these past 6 weeks: the mission of our business and its purpose. Our verse from Matthew 7:12 reminds us how important personal interactions are to entrepreneurs – as we are the face of our company. We reflect the truth of our mission in each interaction we have with others. Will it be an accurate representation of the company? Or will it be an accurate representation of how we are feeling in that moment?

Dear LORD,

Help me this week, to love and reach out to others that You put in my path. Help me to take advantage of each meeting and show others who You are. I pray, Lord, that You would bless the interactions I have with others this week and help me to have eyes to see people as You do. Help me not to be in "work mode" and waste each opportunity in haste because I was more worried about getting on to the "next thing". Help me to take the time needed to treat others the way I would want them to treat me. Show me how to treat others, Lord. Help me to put aside my flesh and any ill emotions I have when I encounter people, and help me instead to minister to them in love and respect.

AMEN

This week, take some time to think of the different people you encounter each day and week. Maybe it's your employees. Maybe your customers. Maybe the service providers you use for your company. Maybe other business owners with whom you network. Consider each encounter and seek to treat them as you would like to be treated.

_____

_____

_____

_____

RESPONSIBILITIES

WHAT RESPONSIBILITIES DO
YOU HAVE AS A BUSINESS
OWNER AND AS A COMPANY?

These next 11 weeks,
focus on each of the
responsibilities you have
in your company. As
entrepreneurs, we are
notorious for wearing
many hats within our
businesses. Sometimes
we run the cash register
or complete transactions
with our customers.

Sometimes we stock the shelves and work the inventory. Other times, we may be the information tech and work out problems with our computers and digital devices or platforms. We may even do the marketing for our business or create the social media content.

"Jesus replied, 'Love the Lord your God with all your heart and with all your soul and with all your mind.' This is the first and greatest commandment. And the second is like it: 'Love your neighbor as yourself.'"

Matthew 22:37-39

This week, specifically, let's look at the attitude we are to have as we carry out each responsibility within our businesses.

With each task that demands your time, skill, and attention, think about how you can show your love for God and your "neighbor" (those He puts in your path).

Dear LORD,

With every responsibility I have, help me to love You first – with all my heart, soul, and mind – so I can love my neighbor as myself. Help me not to have a divided heart. Help me not to prioritize my work responsibilities over my time with You, in prayer, and reading Your Word. Help me to put You first in my life, then my family, and then my work. Help me to be wholly devoted to You so I won't strive after this world that's temporary and destined to burn. Help my mind to not get bogged down and distracted over vain and unimportant things. Help me fulfill my responsibilities and still have time for rest.

AMEN

List some responsibilities you have with your work or business and pray about how you can love God and others while fulfilling each responsibility.

_____

_____

_____

_____

_____

_____

"In the same way,
let your light shine
before others, that
they may see your
good deeds and
glorify your Father
in heaven."

Matthew 5:16

This verse begins, "In the same way,..." What way? The verses just before it explain that you don't light a lamp and hide it. You set it on a stand to shine. Light is meant to shine, not be hidden. Don't be ashamed or shy or fearful to let your light shine at work and through your daily interactions in your business. This is not to draw attention to ourselves or our skills, talents, or achievements. Matthew 5:16 is addressing our words, actions, attitudes, and behaviors before others.

What words do you use to speak about others you work with? Do you gossip about other employees or other customers? Do you use your words to witness for Christ and show kindness to others?

What actions do you show others in and through your business? Are you sloppy and impatient? Or do you work hard as unto the Lord?

What attitudes and behaviors do you have toward your employees and customers? Do you take out your frustrations on them by being hateful and unwilling to work out situations? Or do you take captive every thought unto the Lord and treat others as you would want to be treated?

There are so many things we may encounter day-in and day-out of our work life that we are unable to control. Our response can make a difference in someone's life, possibly even eternally. Let's choose to let our light shine for Christ so that others can see His light through our deeds and give praise and glory to God!

Dear LORD,

I pray You give me boldness at work to let Your light shine to those I meet and interact with each day. Help me not to shy away from witnessing about You. Help me also not to cave to societal pressure and cultural norms around me. Instead, help me to stand firm on Your Word. I pray for divine appointments with my coworkers and customers. I pray I will have opportunities to share the reason I have Your light to shine. And Lord, I pray for protection from the enemy who seeks to put my light out. The enemy wants to diminish my light and make it fade. The enemy will try to pull the shades on my light through difficult customers and complex situations I may encounter at work. Help me to have a right attitude with each trial that comes my way. Help me to not lose my joy, but instead be an example of how Your light cannot be hidden. Your light is a reflection of You and the joy You give us. I pray You give me strength to shine – even on the rainy days!

AMEN

This week, think about the people you encounter each day at work or through your company. Who do you get to talk to? Who do you get to see and physically interact with? Who do you send emails to? Who will observe your behavior and work this week?

"Commit your work
to the LORD, and
then your plans
will succeed."

Proverbs 16:3

Notice the order of steps here. We commit our work to Him, and He will help our plans succeed. The success of those plans is not in our power. All we can do is the work, and the results are left to God. Isn't that a relief?! But what is our normal mode of operation? We strive for the success of the plans and forsake the work, or offload the work, or try to get around the work. The result is not favorable.

So, step 1: We commit our work to the Lord. Committing our work to the Lord shows our dependence on Him. God doesn't expect anything more than your best effort. He knows what you're capable of. That's why we are told to "work as if we are working for the Lord." We do the best we can, staying faithful to the work before us. That's our responsibility. Step 2 belongs to the Lord.

Step 2: And then your plans will be established. Maybe we don't know what to do to help our business grow. We just know we want it to grow and succeed. As we commit our work to God, He will establish those plans we've been mulling over in the back of our minds. He is wise and He has already gone before us. He knows what needs to happen and take place. He has worked out all the details, so He is best to establish those plans.

Does that mean that just because you work and stay faithful to the task before you, God will make all your dreams for your business come true immediately? No. He's not a genie. He's not Santa Claus. This verse is not something we proclaim as if we had some power over Him.

Your "plans will succeed" and your "thoughts are established" because you are focused on the work in front of you. You are working each task as it comes, not getting ahead of yourself. You are working in an honest manner, paying an honest wage, and committing each task's completion to the Lord. You are not distracted with dreaming and making money. You are doing the next task before you, depending on the Lord for the future and details of the plans you've been dreaming about.

The world tells us to strive and hustle, becoming slaves to our business and careers, and forsaking our family and faith. But our verse this week contains rest. When we commit our work to the Lord, we can rest in Him to establish our plans.

Dear Lord,

Help me to commit my work to You. With each task I have to complete this week, help me to do my best and not get distracted with the plans and dreams I have for my company. Help me to stay faithful to the work I have, and to be thankful I am employed, and have the opportunity to do what I love. Lord, strengthen me on those days I am tempted to get weary of the work and begin to long for those future plans and dreams I have for my business. Equip me for the work ahead, Lord; and give me wisdom and discernment with decisions that will impact the future of my company. Help me not to get ahead of You, Lord. Help me to leave the results to You, Lord, because I cannot control everything. Help me to continue trusting in You for the things to come in the future of my business. Help me to continue faithfully committing my work to You. I can't wait to see how You establish the plans! Help me to be patient as You work out the details in Your perfect timing. Teach me in the process and show me Your hand of involvement while I wait for the plans to be established. Thank You for bearing fruit in my life and the life of this company.

Amen

This week, think about your projected plans and future ideas for your company. Think about those dreams you have for your business and the new products you hope to develop or services you want to offer. Take a few minutes and jot them down. Make a quick list to glance over as you pray and read through Proverbs 16:3.

_____

_____

_____

_____

_____

_____

_____

_____

_____

_____

_____

"A just balance and scales belong to the Lord; all the weights of the bag are His concern."

Proverbs 16:11

Fair and honest business dealings are of utmost importance to the Lord. Me makes it His business. Seek Him to help guide you as you set prices for your products and services. Ask Him to give you wisdom as you set a value for each item you offer to customers.

Pray also for protection from vendors and suppliers that you work with, and that God will protect you from being the victim of their unjust, unfair, or dishonest expenses. Ask God for eyes to see through unsafe trades and business deals.

As a business, we have the responsibility of doing right by our customers. We example Christ even through the money we charge for our products and services. Therefore, we should be honest, reliable, fair, and display integrity in all our business dealings.

As employees, we have the responsibility of taking action when we are aware of dishonest gains. Let us be bold to stand for truth and justice and not take part in any evil that our employer is doing. This action and stand we take may even include our leaving for alternate employment. May God guide us if and when that were to occur – to know the timing and to rely on Him for provision and future employment.

Dear LORD,

Thank You for the opportunity You give us to provide products and services to our customers. Give us wisdom and discernment as we place a value to these and assign a cost to our products. Help us not be tempted to falsely advertise or deceive our buyers in any way. Help us to be honest and fair. Lord, we also ask for Your protection as we engage with vendors and suppliers. Help us not to be taken advantage of or fall victim to false advertising or dishonest gain. Help us to be fully aware of any schemes or deceptive tricks that may try to cause extravagant or unnecessary expenses. Help us to have Your eyes to see through the smoke and mirrors and have the knowledge to fully investigate each offer before committing to any purchase or subscription.

AMEN

This week, consider the business deals and transactions that go on in your company with your suppliers, vendors, contractors, and customers. Remember that God is concerned with fair business dealings with each transaction we make, each contract we sign, and each project we commit to completing. He sees all that goes on above and under the table. Nothing escapes His awareness.

_____

_____

"He must labor, performing with his own hands what is good, so that he will have something to share with one who has need."

Ephesians 4:28

We are to be charitable, giving even out of the little we have earned. Charitable giving is not just for the rich. It's for every one of us. We often think it's just the work of a philanthropist, but our verse this week shows us it's for you and me too – those of us who labor.

It is good that we share with those who have need. It gets us outside ourselves. We begin to hold loosely what could so easily strangle us. We need to be master over our resources and not let them be master over us. When we share with others in need, it is one way we display that we control our resources, and not the other way around.

Dear LORD,

Help us to labor and not steal. Help us to work hard with our hands and bodies to do what is good. Help us to be fruitful with our time and schedules so that we can produce a harvest that can be shared with others in need. Help us not to be stingy with what You bless us with. Help us to pour open the gates and give generously and freely as You lead us. Help us to remember that all we have is because of You, anyway. You are the One who gave us the skills and minds to do what we do. You gave us the abilities we have. You gave us strength in our bones and muscles and brains to be able to produce what we do. You give us our reward. Help us to be grateful for what You have done and to give unto others out of the thanksgiving we have toward You. Thank You Lord for Your provisions. Thank You for the many blessings You have given us. Help us to be good stewards of those blessings and to use them to bless others. Open our eyes and give us divine guidance as to when to share them and who to share them with. Show us how, Lord.

AMEN

This week, think about why we work. Consider the purpose of our work and the benefits it provides, not only ourselves, but also others. We are called to work – to provide for our own needs, but not just that. It is not just a means to an end. Our work is not to be only for our own profit, but to enable us to help others.

"He who tills his land
will have plenty of
bread, but he who
pursues vain things
lacks sense."

Proverbs 12:11

In Bible times, farmers had a keen understanding of their land and the seasons in which they till, plant, and harvest – at just the right time. The tilling and planting were crucial to having a good harvest. And they depended on each harvest to provide food for their families. But there were fools then, just as now. The fools would forsake the tilling and planting, and instead would chase fantasies like obtaining unlawful gain or placing hopes in discovering treasure.

In our world today, some of us pursue employment, others work at home and care for their families. But the foolish people leave these obligations uncompleted while they waste time chasing unimportant things or playing the lottery. They forsake the good, hard, honest work and instead put their time and the only money they have into dreams that never provide a sustainable future.

As we do the hard work the Lord has set before us, we will be satisfied in Him. And we will enjoy the fruit of our labor, under God's blessing.

When we live for vain things and chase fantasies, we will lack more than just bread and income, we will lack understanding. We will have no sense, as our verse this week tells us.

Dear LORD,

Help me to have wisdom and discernment to do the work You have called me to. Help me to work diligently at my work so I can reap the fruit of my labor. Help me not to get sidetracked and distracted with vain things that the world throws at me. Help me not to waste time chasing fantasies and ignoring Your direction. Guide me Lord, in the work of my hands and mind. Guide my work so that it is what I am supposed to be doing and what I'm supposed to focus my mind and efforts on. Take away those things that seek to pull me off the path You have for me. And protect me, Lord, from those who would try to entertain itching ears with dreams and fantasies that waste time and money and that are not for me. Protect me from "get-rich-quick" schemes and other deceiving paths that seek to pull me away from the more important work that I have to do. Surround me with like-minded entrepreneurs and friends who will encourage me in Your Word and pray for me and push me on to the hard, honest, and good work that is before me.

AMEN

This week, think about the type of work you do. Think about the services your business may provide. Over and over in God's Word, we find Him pointing to the benefits of work – good, honest, hard work. But our verse this week shows a specific kind of work. Work that is productive and does not foolishly waste time.

"But you are to
remember the Lord
your God, for it is
He who is giving you
power to make wealth,
in order to confirm
His covenant which He
swore to your fathers,
as it is this day."

Deuteronomy 8:18

Be humble. Our power comes from God.

By remembering God as the Source of our provision, we protect our hearts. Our success has the potential to corrupt our hearts. The way to protect against pride in a blessed life is found in our verse this week, and it starts with remembering. It is to remind us not to trust in riches. Riches come and go, but the Lord is faithful and endures forever. Our faith and hope and trust is in the Source – our Lord and Savior.

When we experience success in our work, we are quick to take credit and attribute the success to our hands that made or our minds that had the knowledge. But it's God who gave us the talent and ability to do what we do.

Our gifts and talents weren't given to us by God so that we would only make money or be successful at our job. He blesses us so that we will glorify Him and fulfill the work of His Kingdom. He gives us power to earn wealth so "He may confirm His covenant."

Dear Lord,

Help me to remember it is You who has given me the talents and abilities I have and with which I am able to employ for a financial return. Thank You, Lord, for giving me strong hands to work and a mind that is tuned to the task You have set before me to do. Help me to use well and wisely the power You give me to earn any wealth. Keep me humble, Lord; and remind me constantly that You are the Source of my skill and talent. Help me to continuously give credit to You and point others back to You whenever they compliment my work or reward me for my skills and talents. May I always seek to lift You up in my work, and to give generously from what You have so graciously given to me.

Amen

This week, consider your gifts, talents, and skillsets. Think about all the things you can do. What are your capabilities? At what point in your life did you decide to do what you do for a living? What things contributed to your learning? Who mentored you? What college degree(s), certifications, or licenses did you achieve? When we are profitable in our work and find that "business is good", it is easy to forget Who gave us the ability to work and earn that profit.

"Poor is one who works
with a lazy hand,
But the hand of the
diligent makes rich."

Proverbs 10:4

When we work with lazy hands, we will not receive substantial or sustaining return. The effort we put forth immediately impacts what is earned. When we give minimal, we get back minimal.

On the other hand, when we are diligent in our work and put out earnest effort, we are compensated accordingly. Our verse this week even says we are made "rich."

Rich doesn't only have financial implications, but also implies spiritual richness. Laziness in our spiritual life can bring spiritual poverty, but those who are diligent in their Christian walk, keeping a fervent spirit, will be rich in faith and in good works.

Dear Lord,

Help me not to be sloppy, lazy, or negligent in my work. Help me to get enough rest and not be overwhelmed, so I can put forth my best effort. Help me to work diligently, earnestly putting my hands and mind to the work You have given me to do. When I am tempted to take shortcuts, remind me that I will receive what my work was worth. Encourage me Lord, when the work is long, tiring, and hard. Help me to not give up. Help me to faithfully employ my hands and mind to produce and create for my business what will benefit it as well as the customers who receive the end product.

Amen

This week, consider the time you spend working. How many hours do you log a week at your company? How many days a week do you work? What hours is your business open? How much time do you spend in production? How many hours do you spend providing the service you sell? It's hard to make money when you're not working. If you have nothing to sell or offer for service, then it's pretty hard to make any money or receive anything in return. But our verse this week even defines how the work is done, which affects our reward.

_____

_____

_____

"The lazy one does
not plow after the
autumn, so he begs
during the harvest
and has nothing."

Proverbs 20:4

It's easy to come up with a million excuses as to why we aren't working. But all that procrastinating is just delaying our progress and potential success. It's a principle that can be applied to many areas of our lives and not only our careers.

Every day we put off doing the work we were called to do, we are delaying the fruit of that labor and the blessings that come with it. We can begin by just taking one step today, and tomorrow doing it again, and then adding another step, and before long, you will have made weeks' and months' worth of progress. But it all begins with work. We have to start and we have to continue, not slacking or only putting in half the work for half the year.

Even when business is slow or closed for whatever reason, there is always work to be done. Maybe it's maintenance issues. Maybe it's accounting. Maybe it's planning for the next year. Maybe it's reviewing current practices and making changes and adjustments to better fit your company. Maybe it's a new marketing plan. Or maybe it's adjustments with your staff. There's always something that can be done in the life of your business and to the betterment of your future success.

Dear LORD,

Your Word tells me that I will reap what I sow. So help me to continue sowing, and tending, and working. Help me not to be tempted to pause my work for an extended period of time and fail to ensure a future harvest. Give me strength for my work through the year so I can have a harvest. Protect me from the lazy attitude that tells me to put things off. Stir up in me an attitude of perseverance so that I will continue producing in the "off-seasons" of my company. Keep me from the temptation to quit or take it easy when business is slow. Keep me from the temptation to think my work is finished when I have received a bountiful harvest.

AMEN

This week, focus on your business plan. Do you have a yearly planning meeting? Do you set goals for marketing? Do you have a budget? Consider the preparation you do for your company before a new product launch or a new marketing campaign. If you want it, you gotta work for it! Just like being fit for summer starts in the winter, if we want to do well year-round then we need to be working toward that end each month, and not only seasonally.

_____

_____

_____

"...learn to engage in good deeds to meet pressing needs, so that they may not be unfruitful."

Titus 3:14

Sometimes in our quest for financial security, we end up ignoring the needs of others, and sacrificing time with our families and friends. When really, we should be employing ourselves in good and right things so we can provide for the needs of others, be present with our families, and serve the Lord.

In the NIV, Titus 3:14 is put like this: "Our people must learn to devote themselves to doing what is good, in order to provide for urgent needs and not live unproductive lives."

Dear LORD,

Help me to devote myself to doing what is good. Show me the good and right things I am to do each week, and help me to stay productive. Show me areas where I can do better so I can provide for urgent needs. Bring to my awareness those who have urgent needs so I can step out in obedience and assist when and where needed. Give me wisdom and discernment as I reach out to help. And give me a generous spirit so I will joyfully provide for needs out of love, and not begrudgingly or out of obligation. Bear fruit in my life as I live surrendered to You, Lord. Guide me in my work and help me as I make decisions about my job each day and each week. Help me to be sensitive to Your Holy Spirit and to pay attention, not straying from the path You have for me.

AMEN

This week, focus on the purposes of your job. What does your job do for you? What does it do for others? What difference has it made in the lives of those around you? Do you have any testimonials? Do you receive any positive reviews? One of the purposes for our occupations is to provide us the opportunity to meet pressing needs within the body of Christ and to keep us productive in our faith, so we won't be unfruitful in the works of the Lord.

_____

_____

"The beginning
of wisdom is:
Acquire wisdom;
And with all your
possessions, acquire
understanding."

Proverbs 4:7

Our verse this week gives us a two-step plan: First we acquire wisdom, then we get understanding.

Oftentimes, we regard money or success as the principle thing, but our verse this week reminds us that we should give a higher place to wisdom. It is the principle thing.

Instead of getting distracted with all the doing and going, we should spend time in prayer asking the Lord for wisdom. He is the Source of wisdom and He promises to give it to all who ask. Seek Him for His wisdom and discernment in the crucial decisions of your company, as well as guidance even in the small decisions you make day-to-day.

He's already gone before us. He knows before we do. He is Sovereign and able to orchestrate details in ways we never can. Trust Him in the process and wait for His instruction. He will give you understanding.

Dear LORD,

Help us to learn wisdom. Instead of being tempted to rely on others and their earthly wisdom, help us to rely on Your wisdom. Help us to develop wisdom. When we get lazy in our understanding, help us to not give up or settle but to invest in and work toward the growth of the wisdom You give us. Help us also to obtain wisdom through the people You place in our path to help us in our businesses. Help us to discern the right wisdom and to know when to hold back or get a second opinion. Help us to desire wisdom more than acquiring money or fame. Be with us in every decision that arises within our jobs and give us the wisdom to choose the correct option. Grant us favorable outcomes through these wise decisions.

AMEN

This week, as we come to a close on the topic of responsibilities, think about the wisdom that is needed as we fulfill the tasks that lay before us. Think about the decisions you've had to make in the early stages of your company. What about the decisions you've had to make during the years of crisis in our nation or in your own life personally. Do you make decisions every day on your job? What are some of the heavier decisions you've had to make that required the wisdom of others?

_____

_____

DEPENDENCE

FOR
PROVISION

Who do you depend on to do their job within your company? Who do you place your trust in to provide what's needed? Some of us are a "one-man (or woman) show" and some of us have a staff that assists in the day-to-day operations of our business. We depend on people inside our workplace as well as outside. But there is only One who is able to make provision for us; He is the Source of our provision.

Over the next 12 weeks, we're going to spend some time thinking about God's provision and thanking Him for the ways He provides for our businesses and jobs. May these next few months be a time to return our hearts to a dependence on the Lord to do and provide in ways we cannot do for ourselves.

"I am the vine; you
are the branches.
If you remain in me
and I in you, you
will bear much fruit;
apart from me you
can do nothing."

John 15:5

We can't bear fruit alone. Without Christ, we can do nothing. We can't be fruitful when we're living outside God's will. We need to focus on remaining near to Christ – abiding in Him. As we abide in Him, staying close by His side, we will bear fruit. And as we bear fruit, we inherently have the potential to plant seeds – just as plants in our natural world work to reproduce themselves and make more. We have the potential to plant seeds of the Gospel in our every encounter.

But again, this happens as we remain in Christ. He is the One who gives eternal value to the things we do. He is the One who grows the fruit. Without Him, our works cannot accomplish what His strength and power are capable of doing.

Dear LORD,

You have made everything possible for me to operate my business. You have given me the skills I need to be successful in my endeavors. You have provided me with a support system of family and friends who encourage me in my work. You provide the opportunity for a transaction, and it's You who gives me the successful sale each week. You make it possible for me to do what I do. Help me, Lord, to remember that nothing is possible on my own. I want to rely on You with every step I take in my business. I want to depend on You, daily, for provision and guidance in the decisions I make. Thank You for the freedoms I have in my country to own and operate my own company. May I never forget that You are the vine and I am just a branch. Cut off from You, we lose the live-giving sustenance we need. Help me to bear fruit so I can have the opportunity to plant seeds in others. Help me to abide in You and Your Word so I can bear fruit in each season. Help my company to bear fruit for You.

AMEN

This week, specifically, take some time to consider how God has made everything possible and that without Him, nothing would be possible in our life, our work, our family, and our world.

_____

_____

"For the Lord gives
wisdom; from
his mouth come
knowledge and
understanding."

Proverbs 2:6

The Lord gives wisdom, so let's ask for it. Ask Him for His help as you navigate business decisions. He provides the knowledge. When we don't know the answer, He does. He also provides the understanding. He gives us a discerning heart so we will know how our choices affect others. He has already gone before us in our business venture. He knows what the market will do before Wall Street does. He knows the result of our choices before they are even made.

We need to see the value of His wisdom, knowledge, and understanding as higher than any worldly thing we're offered. The world is only wise in its own ways. But God's ways are above the ways of the world. He has a wisdom the world does not know. And He offers that wisdom to us. Why would we not tap into that wealth of resources!

Dear LORD,

Build my knowledge of the business world. Build my knowledge of technology so I can run my business efficiently and successfully, utilizing all the resources available to me. Help me, Lord, to have greater understanding of marketing and how best to reach my customers. Give me understanding as I seek to create and design products that will be encouraging and useful for my customers. Help me to know the best decision to make when faced with critical junctions in my company. Grow me, Lord, and stretch me outside my comfort zone so I will learn to continually lean on You for understanding. Help me to never get too prideful that I think I know all there is to know about business. Our world is changing every day, and every year it seems there are different hoops to jump through. Lord, give me strength to persevere through the unknowns and to depend on You for wisdom so I can get through it all.

AMEN

This week, ask the Lord to give you greater knowledge and understanding of your business – its market sector, your customer base, things you need to upgrade, changes that need to be made to your business structure. And ask Him for wisdom as you apply what you learn.

_____

_____

"I can do all things
through Him who
strengthens me."

Philippians 4:13

Maybe it all feels too much.
Maybe it overwhelms you just
thinking about the long list in
front of you. Our verse this week
reminds us that it is too much,
it is overwhelming – in our own
strength. But through Christ, and
His strength – we can finish.

Christ is our Source of power and
strength. He helps us endure all
things – the good and the bad. The
easy and the hard. The simple and
the complex. All things, we can do
through Christ because it is He who
gives us strength to do them.

Dear LORD,

Thank You for Your strength. Help me to remember that it is only through You that I am able to do the things I need to do with my job. You give me strength to do my work. I can't do all things on my own. I need You. I pray You give me Your strength with the work I have before me this week. The customer interactions, the planning meetings, the vendor contracts, the marketing, the product designs, the content to write and send out. All the things, Lord. I can't do them on my own. But through You, I can accomplish much. Your strength is more than my weakness. Through You, I can have victory over my to-do list. Through You and the strength You give me, I can do all the things I need to do. Help me to always remember this – especially on those difficult days when I feel so small, inept, and overwhelmed.

AMEN

This week, think about all the things you have to do for your work. All the projects that are yet to be completed. All the tasks that await you each day. All the people and meetings and schedules and obligations that must be fulfilled this week. And ask the Lord to give you His supernatural strength to complete the work that is set before you.

"When I am
afraid, I will
trust in You."

Psalm 56:3

Although God's Word tells us over and over again, "Do not fear," the psalmist acknowledges our human weakness to be afraid. But our verse this week gives us a course of action, a step of obedience – we are to trust in God.

It's often easier said than done to trust when we are most fearful. Maybe it's an inevitable outcome that we cannot reverse. Maybe it's an unknown outcome that we fear the worst. Perhaps the trouble is due to our mistakes. Or perhaps the calamity was brought on us unknowingly.

Whatever it is that is causing you to be afraid in your business and respond in fear and anxiety over your work, don't let it stop you from trusting in God. He is our anchor through every storm. We need to hold fast to Him and He will carry us through – no matter what comes. He will walk through the fire with us and guide us each step of the way.

Because we are in Him, we need not fear. Because He is God, we shall not fear. He is always greater than our troubles. Whatever you're going through this week or this year in your company that may incite fear and anxiety within you, keep trusting in the One who is still in control.

Dear Lord,

I pray that You hold me in Your perfect peace when I am tempted to fear and become anxious. When there are things I cannot control in my job. When there are people who threaten my peace. When there are changes and situations that cause me to be afraid. Lord, help me to always trust in You – through it all. Lord, remove my fear and replace it with Your peace, the peace that surpasses understanding. Lord, remove my anxious thoughts and help me to remember You are still in control and nothing catches You by surprise. Nothing throws You off or makes You worry. Remind me of Your truth when I am overwhelmed with circumstances that have unknown outcomes. Hold me tightly and surround me with Your presence. Bring to mind the truth found in Your Word. Lift my head and help me to focus my eyes and mind on You as I trust in You.

Amen

What are the things making you anxious this week with your business? What worries you about your job? What keeps you awake at night or fills your mind during the day while you work? Is there a fear you've been battling? This week, focus on this verse and remind yourself as often as needed, to trust in the Lord.

_____

_____

"Trust in the LORD with all your heart, and do not rely on your own understanding; in all your ways know him, and he will make your paths straight."

Proverbs 3:5-6

Trust Him with all your heart. That implies totality. We are to trust Him wholly. Seeking Him in everything we do. We are not to rely on our own understanding. Why? Because we don't know everything.

In all our ways, we are to "know Him." That means to be aware of Him at all times, in all things. And what is the result? That He will "make your paths straight." He will guide you.

It's wise to discern what our focus ought to be and to filter out any activities that don't align. We don't have to take advantage of every single opportunity just because it comes along. In fact, we shouldn't say "yes" to every opportunity if we want to avoid burnout.

Dear LORD,

Help me to let go of the things in my work that I cannot control. Help me to trust You in every area of my business. The sales, the customers, the product lines, the marketing, and especially the finances. Lord, I confess, I don't have all the answers, but I know You do. I am seeking You for guidance in the decisions of my company. I ask for Your wisdom and discernment as opportunities are presented to me. Help me know which activities I am to engage in and which ones I am to let go of, and decline involvement. Help me not to be rash or act in haste, but instead take my time and seek You for counsel first. Make my paths straight, Lord.

AMEN

Are there things in your work you are trying to control? Are there things you are struggling with in your business that need wisdom and direction? This week, give up control and let God be your guide.

_____

_____

_____

_____

_____

_____

"Can any of you
add one moment
to his life span by
worrying? If then
you're not able to
do even a little
thing, why worry
about the rest?"

Luke 12:25-26

It seems inevitable that if you haven't worried about some part of your job, you soon will. The days and weeks seem to ebb and flow with good moments and bad. And the things we worry about within our companies also seem to ebb and flow, as some concerns are relieved and others go unresolved.

But as our verse this week reminds us, we really cannot control or ensure "even a little thing." Therefore, we are encouraged not to worry "about the rest." This verse makes it sound like a simple task, but reality and life seem to show the difficulty involved.

Our worry stems from the constant reminder that we are but dust. So many things overwhelm us because we can't control people, situations, or outcomes. And that's precisely the reason the Lord tells us not to worry. Worrying has no benefit to our lives. It's like a rocking chair. We do a lot of "moving", but we never get anywhere or gain any ground.

We may not know the future, or how people will act, or what the outcomes may be, but one thing we can be sure of is God's providence: His foreseeing care and guidance. He promises to take care of His children. He promises to be with us. He offers us His wisdom, but also His listening ear. He willingly offers His shoulders to carry our concerns and burdens. So whatever has you worried this week with your job, the work ahead of you, the viability of your business, and the current or future state of your company – give it to the Lord.

Dear LORD,

Help me not to worry about the things I cannot control. Help me not to expend energy, wasting time worrying about "what if". Help me not to be overwhelmed with the unknown. Instead, Lord, help me to trust You with all these concerns. Strengthen my faith and keep my feet firmly planted in You and Your Word. Remind me of Your truths and encourage me this week to continue trusting in You. Protect me from the enemy and the thoughts he tries to plant in my mind that push me toward worrying. Thank You for Your providence, Lord. Thank You for Your care of me and my business and the guidance You give me. Help me to quiet my heart and my mind so I can hear Your direction. Give me peace in my mind and calm those anxious thoughts.

AMEN

What's been on your mind this week? What are you worrying over with regards to your business? Is it workers? Is it the future of your company? Is it finances? Is it having work to do? Whatever those worries are, give them to the Lord. Leave them with Him and trust that they are in His capable hands.

"Cast your burden
on the LORD, and
He will sustain
you, He will never
allow the righteous
to be shaken."

Psalm 55:22

This verse is so simple and we may have heard it or read it a million times, but let's break down and look at some of the key words in this verse.

"Burden" – what the Lord has given you; what He has allowed to come to you.

"Righteous" – morally upright, just, lawful, godly, or virtuous.

"Shaken" – to totter or move in a feeble or unsteady way; to slip and fall.

"Sustain" – to carry, or take care of.

The Lord doesn't cause your burdens, but He allows them to come into your life. Even so, He is still in control. He will not leave you. He will take care of you, sustain you, and help you to remain upright and strong in your faith.

Don't allow the overwhelming thoughts to take up any more space in your mind. Give them to the Lord and He will take care of you. Whatever it is you have been burdened with – go to God in prayer and ask Him to help you. Ask Him to sustain you. Ask him to hold you up. Invite the Lord into your business. Invite Him into your financials, your marketing plans, your customer sales, your product ideas and how they are carried out.

Dear LORD,

You already know what my burdens are. You see me up at night when I am worried about my company. You already know the thoughts I have before they've even come to be. And You've also already gone before me. Please, Lord, sustain me and don't allow me to be shaken. Help me with the burdens I have in my work. I want to give them to You. Help me not to hang onto them or feel like I am the only one to take care of them and deal with them. I need Your intervention. I need Your strength. I want to . let my burdens loose by directing them to You. And when I let them go, help me to not be tempted to pick them back up.

AMEN

What burdens are you facing this week? What has your stomach in knots? What keeps you up at night? What consumes your thoughts during the day? This week, whatever it is your business is facing, cast those cares, concerns, and burdens onto the Lord. Give them to Jesus.

_____

_____

_____

_____

_____

"Now if any of you lacks wisdom, he should ask God - who gives to all generously and ungrudgingly - and it will be given to him."

James 1:5

We are told to ask God for His wisdom. Why? Because we are deficient in wisdom. We don't always have all the answers. We don't always know what to do or how to respond. There are things we need help with. And when we ask God, He responds without reproach or faultfinding. He gives us wisdom because He wants to and enjoys doing it. He already knows what we need. He's expecting us to come to Him and ask.

Dear LORD,

Humble me in my work. Humble my heart and mind so I will approach You and ask for Your wisdom. I need to know how to proceed with my company. Help me to know what products to launch and when. Help me to know the pricing of my products. Help me with the marketing of those products and to know whether or not to pay for ad space. Help me know how best to serve my clients. Help me to know how to provide for my customers in the best way possible. I don't want to check with You as an afterthought. I want to seek You first for wisdom before I act. Help me to have ears to hear Your instruction and to have obedience to follow through. Give me faith to respond and help me to trust You with the decisions I have to make in my business.

AMEN

What do you need God's wisdom for this week? What part of your business do you help with? What decisions lay before you this week? This year? Ask God. He gives His wisdom to you freely. He will not rebuke you for asking Him.

_____

_____

_____

_____

"I will instruct you
and show you the
way to go; with my
eye on you, I will
give you counsel."

Psalm 32:8

Oftentimes, we can confide in others to give us advice or counsel us with decisions in our business. But many times, it's just a one-time consultation. We don't refer to them with every question that arises or call them every minute we run into a dilemma. And so they may not have a vested interest in our company or its success.

But our verse this week reminds us that God is very interested in our life, our business, and the direction we are to take. And it's so much so that our verse says He will not only instruct us, but He will also show us. He even goes so far as to say how He will do this: with His "eye on you." Wow!

God says He will guide us along the best pathway for our life. He not only advises us, He also watches over us. And it's not just a generic direction. You know, some people will advise us, but it's just in the general direction we should turn our attention to. Not so with God. Our verse above says He shows us "the way" – He's very specific. He makes us wise as He shows us which way to go. We can count on Him to never lead us astray. His counsel can be trusted. He is faithful and true. He will tell us what to do.

Dear LORD,

I pray You help me by instructing me and showing me the way to go in every area of my business. Give me Your eyes to see. Keep Your eye on me and guide me along Your path for my life and my company. Help me seek You before seeking the world or others. Give me a humble and discerning heart to take and apply the instruction You give me. Help me to trust You with the outcome. Help me not to fear all the "what-ifs" that I may be tempted to allow to paralyze me when it comes to making decisions in my business. The only way I am going to be successful and fruitful in my work is if You are the One guiding me, directing me, and showing me the way to go. Thank You for never leading me astray. Thank You that I can trust You because You are always faithful, even when I'm not. Thank You Lord for telling me what to do and how to do it. Thank You for the resources You provide for me.

AMEN

Where do you go for instruction? Who tells you how to do things or which direction to take in your business? Who helps you know where to go? Do you have a mentor for your company? Is there a seasoned employee or friend who helps you? Do you seek out professional entrepreneurs on social media and subscribe or follow their wisdom? Do you rely on Google?

"But godliness
actually is a means
of great gain when
accompanied by
contentment."

1 Timothy 6:6

It's easy to look around and see other businesses thriving and growing and having a huge reach online with social media. It's easy to be overwhelmed with the seeming lack of attention your company is receiving. After awhile, we may find ourselves being tempted to measure our gain by the world's standards. Yes, it is necessary to make a profit in order to pay your bills and make a living. However, we need to be careful that we are not measuring our success through the world's eyes.

Our verse this week tells us godliness is our means of great gain as believers. And not by itself, but when something else accompanies it. What was it? Contentment. Ouch. That's a hard word for some. We often associate being content with settling and not reaching for more. Being content does not mean you "settle". It is not implying you are lacking, or missing, or just accepting the minimal effort and results. Contentment means we are at peace and satisfied. We may not have all we want, but we have all we need.

Look at how the NLT reads for 1 Timothy 6:6 - "Yet true godliness with contentment is itself great wealth." Did you see that? "Great wealth!" Wow! Great wealth is not always measured monetarily.

This is not to say that we cannot earn money or sell goods to make a profit. This is also not to say that we can't make a lot of money, or that we cannot have growth or expansion in our business. What it is saying is that we need to keep a proper perspective. Our desires shouldn't own us. The desire for more money and greater profit should not be our master. We need to master our money and steward it rightly. We are not to fill our life and needs with the materialistic things of the world. We are to fill our life with the eternal things of God. After all, we can take nothing with us when we leave this world. It will all be left behind. And someone else will own it.

Dear LORD,

Help me to have a proper view of any gain I receive in my business. Set my eyes on godliness instead of all the things I think I need or wish I had or could do. Help me to be at peace with my position, and help me seek to make much of You instead of much of me. And when You bless my work, help me to be humble and give You the credit and glory and honor for my success. I want an attitude of gratitude and not a spirit of greed or covetousness. Help me to steward well what You have given me and allowed me the opportunity to have. I want to please You more than my selfish desires. Help me to have a proper perspective of money, and profit, and success. I want Your definition of success and not the world's. Help me not to get distracted with the world's standards and help me to find my worth and value in You.

AMEN

How do you measure great gain? Do you immediately think of it in terms of finances? "Great" gain is the bottom line ever increasing? "Great" gain is the increasing profit of your business? The possible expansion of your company? What will it take to reach your idea of "great" gain? This week, think about God's definition of great gain and how you can rest in Him and be content because of what He has done on your behalf and the provision He has given you.

_____

_____

_____

_____

_____

_____

_____

_____

_____

_____

_____

"Do not weary
yourself to gain
wealth; stop
dwelling on it."

Proverbs 23:4

Weariness is an unhealthy exhaustion. Our world often embraces this and even gives it a pet name: hustle. We're told to hustle in our day job, and when that is done, to go and hustle some more on a side job. There are even energy drinks that try to help us work through the hustling; and it's all just a sad attempt to prevent exhaustion.

We were not made or meant to exhaust ourselves in this way. That's why God set the example in Genesis 2:2. After God created the world and all that was in it, we are told "He rested." He made a special day for the sole purpose of resting. If anyone can work 24/7, 365, it's God. And the Bible tells us in Psalm 121:4 that God never sleeps nor slumbers. But we aren't God. We need to rest.

We can work hard and should – but not to get rich, as our verse this week reminds us. And our verse doesn't stop there. It goes on to say not to even consider it.

Often, when we have success or make a profit, we begin to fixate on making more money; and pretty soon we're in over our heads with a million different ways to chase a dollar. It often ends in overwhelm, and exhaustion, and frustration.

This is not to say that making a profit is bad and it's also not to say we shouldn't try to be successful. The point of the verse this week is to bring awareness to the motive of our heart. We are not to make an idol of wealth. We are not to worship our work. Working hard is wise and encouraged, but living for riches is foolishness. Our focus should be set higher – on eternal things, not the temporary pleasures of this world.

Dear LORD,

Help me this week to not weary myself to gain wealth. Help me to rest from my work and find refreshing strength from Your Word. I want to seek You for help with the things that overwhelm me and that are out of my control. Set my eyes on things above – the eternal things that matter more than this earth that is passing away. Help me not to make an idol out of my work. I want my work to be a way for me to reach others for Your Kingdom. And I want my work to be one way for me to meet needs and be a blessing to others. I don't want my work to master me or tempt me to chase after wealth.

AMEN

Are you weary? Are you worn out? Are you waiting for relief or maybe just for this season in your business to pass? As an entrepreneur, there are many things that can cause us to become weary or worrisome. This week, let's consider casting our weary thoughts and anxieties onto the Lord, and find rest in Him.

_____

_____

_____

_____

_____

"For what does it
benefit a person
to gain the whole
world, and forfeit
his soul?"

Mark 8:36

We may grow our business from the ground up. We may win awards and make hundreds of thousands of dollars in revenue. We might even make a name for ourselves in our community or state. We may do all these things, but our verse this week cautions us against putting all our eggs in this earthly basket we call life. This week, let's consider our eternal future because one day we will leave this earth. If we don't have our eternity secured in Christ, then what is any of it worth?

Our jobs can't save our souls. Our businesses doesn't get us into heaven. We need to make sure we are not placing our jobs over our salvation. Instead, we work "out of" or "from" our salvation. Our security in Christ helps us govern our actions and set our priorities. After all, when we leave this earth, we can't take our work or our business with us. We will leave it all behind.

So we need to be good stewards of what we've been given, but not worship it or make it our idol. Our work should not take us away from Christ. Instead, our closeness to Christ should motivate us to have a right view of the things in our life.

Nothing in this world is worth going to hell for. Nothing!

Dear LORD,

Help me to have a right view of life, and work, and the things that constitute living on this earth. Help me not to get swept away trying to live for this world that is fading away. Help me to have a heavenly mindset that is focused on eternity.

AMEN

If you have not placed your faith in Jesus Christ, why wait? Call on His Name today for salvation. Confess that you are a sinner and ask Him to forgive you for your sins. He wants to be Lord and Savior of your life!

_____

_____

_____

_____

_____

_____

_____

_____

WORK
ETHIC

HOW WOULD YOU DESCRIBE
YOUR ATTITUDE AT WORK?

WHAT ABOUT YOUR WORK ETHIC?

WOULD YOUR ANSWER BE DIFFERENT IF
YOU WERE ASKED ABOUT THE ATTITUDE
AND WORK ETHIC OF YOUR EMPOYEES?

For the next 11 weeks, we will be focusing on our attitude and our work ethic. Consider how someone might describe your attitude at work. Consider how they would describe the environment of your company.

Our work ethic doesn't just affect us, it affects everyone around us – from the workers, to the customers and vendors.

Are we greeting customers with a warm welcome?

Are we treating our employees with respect?

Are we working responsibly so others do not have to pick up our slack?

"...Instead, whoever wants to become great among you must be your servant, and whoever wants to be first must be your slave – just as the Son of Man did not come to be served, but to serve, and to give his life as a ransom for many."

Matthew 20:26-28

This week, specifically, let's look at the role of a leader; because as entrepreneurs, we naturally step into the position of leading others. Leadership is to be first and foremost an act of service. As leaders, we are to set the example of service and not expect to be served. Christ was our example, as our verse this week reminds us. We need to be like Him.

Sometimes it's easy to get stuck in "work-mode" and get comfortable delegating tasks and ordering people around. We often do it without even thinking about it – it just comes naturally. But what a difference it would make if we could set an example by showing our staff that we are not above serving.

Even serving customers requires humility. We shouldn't expect a sale from our customers or even their loyal business. They could choose other options to provide for their need or service. So out of gratitude to God for their patronage, we should seek ways to serve them.

Dear LORD,

Give me a humble heart to serve You as I serve others in my work. I want to set an example as I serve my employees and my customers. Help me find ways each week to do this well. Help me not to get prideful or selfish or arrogant and resent serving. Help me to serve for the benefit of the other person. As I serve, help me to reflect Your character, Lord.

AMEN

We don't serve because we have to. We serve because we get to. We serve because Christ served us and all mankind with His sacrificial death on the cross. Even in His earthly life, He was always serving others. So let's determine as we lead, to serve. And as we serve, we will point others to Christ.

What would our office environment be like if we took an interest in serving others, besides just our customers?

_____

_____

_____

_____

_____

_____

"Work hard, but not just to please your masters when they are watching. As slaves of Christ, do the will of God with all your heart. Work with enthusiasm, as though you were working for the Lord rather than for people."

Ephesians 6:6

Why do we work hard? To catch the eye of others? To prove ourselves? To make others like us or value us? Living to please others is a never-ending job. We need to give that up and seek to please Christ more. It is impossible to make every person happy and pleased. There will always be customers or clients or people who disagree with us or dislike the way we do something. And not everyone will want to buy our products or use our services.

But if we are working to please Christ in all we do, seeking to do His will above our own, we will find joy in our work and throughout our days. This joy comes from freedom. When we work for Christ in all we do instead of always trying to please man, we are free from the stronghold of people-pleasing. We are relieved of the burden of trying to make everyone happy.

Dear LORD,

Help me to work hard for You - and You alone. Help me seek to please You above all others. Help me to have integrity and to be open and honest in all I do. Help me not be tempted to deceive, hide, or try to manipulate a situation to make me look better. Help me not be tempted to embellish or enhance another's view of me. Help me to be the same in public as I am in private. I want to be free from the temptation to please others. And instead, I want to seek to do right and obey all You have called me to do. Help me to work with enthusiasm in all I do, sharing Your joy with those I meet each day.

AMEN

Who are you when no one's looking? Do you speak and act the same when others are around? This week, our verse makes us think about who we are in the public eye versus our private life. Let's seek to be people of integrity - doing what's right whether others are watching or not.

_____

_____

_____

_____

_____

_____

"Therefore, my beloved, be steadfast, immovable, always excelling in the work of the Lord, because you know that in the Lord your labor is not in vain."

1 Corinthians 15:58

The Lord calls us His "beloved" because we belong to Him. He sees all we do. He knows our hearts and our intentions. When we feel like nothing we do seems to matter, He lovingly reminds us that our time and efforts are not in vain.

We are called to be steadfast and immovable. That means we are to be dedicated and committed to the work He has for us. We are to be faithful to grow in the work the Lord has called us to do. And the reason we can do all of this is because there is a purpose to our work. God gives purpose to our work so we don't ever have to worry about wasting time and energy. Our responsibility is to be steadfast and immovable, excelling in that work. And God's job is to bring the results - the harvest. Leave the heavy lifting to Him.

Dear LORD,

Help me to be faithful to what You've called me to. Help me to be focused on staying committed to the work and excelling in that work. Thank You for handling the results. Thank you that my time, and energy, and efforts are not in vain. It's not wasted because You are with me and involved in every detail. Guide my hands to the work before me. Steady my thoughts and give me strength to do all You have for me to do. Thank You for giving purpose to my work. Help me to have joy each day, knowing that I have been given this job.

AMEN

Do you ever feel like your work is in vain? Do you feel like sometimes you do, and do, and do – yet seem to make no progress? Does it seem like there is no impact or fruit from your efforts? God's Word gives us hope. He assures us that the work we do for Him is never in vain. That's why He tells us to be unwavering in the work we do; being faithful with the work before us. This week, focus on that hope – that your work for the Lord is not in vain and let it motivate you to work with new purpose.

_____

_____

_____

_____

"And also that every man should eat and drink, and enjoy the good of all his labor, it is the gift of God."

Ecclesiastes 3:13

When we receive good from our labor, we need to acknowledge it is the gift of God – and we need to respond with thanksgiving to Him. Don't get caught up in the gifts and forget the Giver!

There is always something good; we need to seek it out – find it and give credit to God. Each day, we can choose to dwell on the good, and count our blessings. We can always find something good that He has given us: a sale, a witnessing opportunity with a customer, an amazing deal with a vendor, a discount for advertising, or loyal employees.

Instead of getting caught up in what hasn't gone well this week or this month, choose instead to direct your eyes and thoughts on what good has come to you. And remember it has come to you as a gift from God. Give Him thanks!

Dear LORD,

Help me to enjoy the good of my labor today. Help me this week to look for the good You have given me. Thank You for the opportunity to reap the rewards of my efforts. Thank You that there is a good result from the time and energy and work that I put in day after day. When I'm having a hard day, remind me of the good I am able to enjoy because of You. I don't want to desire the blessings more than the Blesser. I want to love You, the Giver, more than the gifts. Thank You for Your goodness toward me. Thank You for the rewards I receive from my labor. Help me to not take them for granted.

AMEN

We have a fresh new week before us! We have another opportunity to reap the reward of our work! God wants us to enjoy the good of our labor. Our verse this week says "it is the gift of God." Have you been able to enjoy the good of your work? What's holding you back?

_____

_____

_____

_____

_____

"But as for you,
be strong and do
not give up, for
your work will
be rewarded."

1 Chronicles 15:7

There are many things throughout our day and week that get thrown at us, and it makes it difficult to "be strong." We have issues at home that we simultaneously deal with while trying to run a business. We have difficult customers or complex orders to fill. We may have issues with employees and struggle to maintain peace within the office.

But we are not to give up; and the reason is because it is certain our work will be rewarded. There will be a result from our investment of time and resources. So how do we not give up? How do we prevent being tempted to get frustrated, bitter, or upset because things aren't moving at the pace we think they should be moving?

We need to take our frustrations to the Lord. We need to give Him our concerns. We need to ask Him for His wisdom and discernment with how to proceed, and in what way. We need His strength to cover our weaknesses. We need to depend on Him to help us persevere and endure. He knows what we struggle with, and He wants to help us.

Perseverance produces character and hope. It's practiced by taking action and moving forward. Perseverance is continuing to work and walk and progress with the help of God's power. Endurance is remaining steadfast and staying your course with the help of God's strength. While both require us to put in hard work to keep going, perseverance is the one that bears much fruit within us. Character development and hope require us to put in some effort, but we aren't working alone! God is our source of all help when we are persevering, and He is also the Provider of the hope that will result. So through all stages of our perseverance, we can have the comfort of knowing He is with us!

Dear LORD,

Help me to keep going when I am tempted to quit. Help me to push through the hard days and weeks and lean on You for strength. Help me to continue doing the tasks before me, knowing they will bear fruit. Thank You for walking alongside me. Remind me I am not alone when I feel like I'm the only one putting in the time, effort, and dedication. I want to persevere despite setbacks, roadblocks, or bad attitudes. Fill me with Your joy as I work; and help me hold on to hope as I look forward in anticipation of the reward that is to come.

AMEN

Have you been working hard and waiting for your reward? The longer we wait, the easier it is to become frustrated or tempted to give up. We don't know how much more it takes – money, time, and effort – before we start to see some kind of fruit. But as our verse this week reminds us, we need to be strong and not let our hands be slack; our work will be rewarded. What area of your business do you need to be strong in and not give up?

_____

_____

_____

_____

"Don't worry about anything, but in everything, through prayer and petition with thanksgiving, present your requests to God. And the peace of God, which surpasses all understanding, will guard your hearts and minds in Christ Jesus."

Philippians 4:6-7

Our verses this week contain two words that are all-encompassing, completely comprehensive: "anything" and "everything." We are not to worry about "anything." That pretty much sums up what we are worrying about today and this week. It's included in that one word.

So we are told not to worry about it, but that's not all. We are also told what to do. In "everything", we are to pray and give up to God. "Everything", once again sums up what plagues our mind today and this week. All-inclusive.

There's nothing that troubles us that God doesn't want to hear about. So why is it so hard to give anything and everything to the Lord? Maybe it's because we struggle with giving up control. By worrying, we feel we still have a little bit of control. But we are mistaken. It's actually the other way around. Whatever we are worrying about is really controlling us. It distracts us and takes priority in our mind and we end up dismissing God's nature and providence.

Our verses this week tell us what will happen when we finally give our worries over to the Lord: His peace will guard our hearts and minds. Like a soldier keeping watch, His peace will provide protection from the anxieties that plague our thoughts. When we are tempted to worry, we have an immediate invitation to prayer in these verses.

Dear LORD,

Thank You for reminding me to pray. Take my concerns and worries and intervene for me. Help me to have Your peace. Meet my needs and help to take away what's bothering me this week. I pray Your grace covers me. Lord, help me to stay strong in faith. I want You to be first in my mind – not worry. You provide all my needs. You have kept me every time. Please keep me once more. Help me to make prayer my first response. Remind me to bring everything to You in prayer because You are God and I am not. You are capable, You are my help in time of need, You are my Provider, and there is nothing that concerns me that doesn't concern You.

AMEN

What worries you this week? What's on your mind? What are you losing sleep over? What makes you bite your fingernails? Whatever it is, take it to God. Pray about it. Surrender it to the Lord and ask Him to give you His peace about it.

_____

_____

_____

_____

_____

"Peace I leave with you. My peace I give you. I do not give to you as the world gives. Don't let you heart be troubled or fearful."

John 14:27

Jesus leaves His peace with us. Whatever situation we are facing, we are not facing it alone. When Jesus left this earth and ascended into heaven, He left His Holy Spirit to indwell believers. It's not something that comes and goes. It stays with us. The peace of Christ is also something given to us and remains with us. He gives His peace to us. What a gift!

The world tries to give us peace by patching up our fears and giving us "synthetic" peace, but it's not authentic. It is a fake. It's a knock-off version. The world's peace aims at pacifying our emotions and playing with our minds to make us feel like we have peace. When really, all it does is distract us from our problems and numb our minds so we don't deal with the underlying issue.

The peace of Christ permeates our body, mind, and soul. It is genuine peace that is experienced despite our circumstances. This peace surpasses understanding because it manifests during times that we would normally erupt in panic or despair.

Maybe you have big decisions coming up in your business. Maybe you are facing huge financial issues. Maybe you have legal problems. Perhaps your vendors are not cooperating. Or your sales are down and you are struggling to figure out marketing and product lines or diversifying your services. Whatever it is that is causing you a troubled heart and inciting fear, take it to the Lord and ask Him to give you His peace.

Dear LORD,

I ask You to fill me with Your peace. I pray You leave Your peace with me so it will infiltrate my mind, heart, and thoughts. Lord, help me to have peace knowing You hear my prayers, You know the concerns on my heart, You know what I'm up against and what I am facing this week and this year. Lord, I trust You to intervene and help me with what's troubling my heart and my mind. I pray for peace with business decisions. I pray for peace with my employees. I pray for peace with my vendors. I pray for peace in my customer interactions. I pray You will be with me through this, guiding my thoughts and my heart, and helping me to walk in Your peace. I pray Your peace in me is felt by others as they interact with me. I pray Your peace permeates every area of my life and business.

AMEN

Is there anything troubling you or making you fearful? Do you need peace as you go into this week? There is One who can give us peace and His peace will not look like the manufactured peace the world tries to pass off.

_____

_____

_____

_____

"Haven't I
commanded you:
be strong and
courageous?
Do not be afraid or
discouraged, for the
Lord your God is with
you wherever you go."

Joshua 1:9

When you run your own business, there are many things that can invoke fear. There are many decisions that have to be made, and we fear the unknown. We fear the result of our decisions. We fear the prospect of failure.

But we are commanded to be strong and courageous; and the reason we are told to do so is because of the simple fact that God is with us. His presence in our business and our decisions should give us courage because He is our help. He guides us in all we do and He gives us wisdom to know what steps to take. He helps us to know when to go and when to stop and which way to turn.

His presence also reminds us that whatever is causing us to fear and be discouraged is underneath Him. He is over everything. He is still in control. He is still reigning and sovereign over all.

We can be strong and courageous simply because we are His. As believers, we belong to Him and He has promised to never leave us or forsake us. No matter what we are facing. No matter what our sales are this month. No matter what the reviews say about us.

Where do you need to be strong and courageous in your work? Obey God's command and do not be afraid; He is with you!

Dear LORD,

Help me to be strong in my work, and to be courageous as I put forth my time and energy to complete what I have set out to do. Help me not to be tempted to fear the unknown. Help me not to fear in the area of finances with my company. Help me not to be discouraged in the area of marketing and growing my customer base. Remind me this week that You are with me, day-in and day-out as I engage with customers and serve those who seek my services. Help me to be brave to try things that are outside my comfort zone. Help me not to fear technology or platforms that could be used to enhance my business, how I operate, or advertise and generate sales. Give me Your strength and fill me with confidence, knowing that You are with me wherever I go and wherever my business takes me.

AMEN

Is there an area of your business where you are feeling weak or discouraged? Are you facing something that seems intimidating or undefeatable? God commands us in the Bible to not be afraid because He is with us. In what area of your company do you need His presence this week?

_____

_____

_____

"In all labor
there is profit, But
mere talk leads
only to poverty."

Proverbs 14:23

"A little less talk and a lot more action."
It's more than song lyrics or a fancy
saying. There's actually a Biblical basis
to back it up. When we only talk about
things, things don't get accomplished.
But when we put forth the work toward
a task or idea, there is a result. Is there
something you've been talking about a
lot lately with regards to your business?
Maybe expanding product lines or finding
new ways to advertise? Maybe networking
with other small businesses or learning
new platforms to use to offer your
services? Have you taken the steps to
start implementing these ideas or are
they still on paper?

Be encouraged this week as you read
Proberbs 14:23, and know that there
is profit in your labor. Be committed
to labor and take the steps needed to
progress in your company.

Dear LORD,

Help me to stop talking about all the ideas, and dreams, and goals I have for my business. Instead, help me to take the first step toward those ideas. Show me what to do first and help me be accountable to completing that task. Lord, show me progress along the way and encourage me as I put my hands and feet to action and take the necessary steps toward meeting my goal. Surround me with like-minded individuals who will lift me up and help me to make my dreams a reality. Build unity in my company with my coworkers and help them to be motivated toward the goal as well. Guide me each step of the way, and give me wisdom and discernment when I am met with roadblocks. Protect me from setbacks and any discouragement the enemy tries to throw at me as I take steps of action and obedience.

AMEN

The hardest step is the first step. But we need to challenge ourselves to take all the talk and put feet to action. What's one step you can take this week to make progress on the "talk"?

What goal will you set this week or this month to begin acting on the ideas you have for your business?

What tool can you use, or who do you know who can hold you accountable to complete these steps of action toward your goal?

"The plans of the
diligent certainly
lead to advantage,
but everyone who is
in a hurry certainly
comes to poverty."

Proverbs 21:5

Our verse this week talks about the plans of the diligent. It's important to be diligent in your work. It means you are steadily working, making progress, in an earnest and energetic fashion. It is the opposite of laziness. So the plans made by the diligent people lead to advantage. It is to their advantage because they are not giving up. They are working toward making progress in their work. They are not satisfied with sitting idle and stagnant. The diligent people want growth.

But just because the people are diligent, that does not imply haste. Diligence in our work does not equal being rushed or hurried. Diligence is steady work, not sloppy work. The work of the hurried people comes to poverty. Why? They are not taking the necessary time to consider and exercise wisdom. It's as if no thought is taking place. There is just productivity with an emphasis on quantity and not quality.

When a job is done quickly, but not correctly – it has to be repeated. It was wasted effort. That's not a smart use of resources, time, or effort. So instead of getting in a hurry because a desired result is wanted more than a job well done, we need to calm our anxious thoughts and exercise patience.

Patience is the key to the "advantage" the diligent people have with their plans. Be patient with the process. Keep doing the next right thing and wait for the Lord to bring about the fruit from your labors.

Dear LORD,

Help me to be patient as You are working to bring Your plans to completion. Help me not to act in haste on any decisions that need to be made for my business. Help me not to rush projects, risking their failure, or having to repeat them. Help me have calm thoughts and a calm mind as I diligently work toward the plans I have for my company. Help my employees not to rush their work or be hurried in any transaction. Give me the fruit of patience as I continue doing the next thing and wait for You to bring the desired result. Help me focus on a job well done instead of a bunch of jobs done quickly.

AMEN

Have you made plans for your business? Are you comfortable with the timeline in which these plans will be carried out? Or do you get tempted to rush the plans along and not wait for the process? This week, think about the plans you have made for your company and how you are doing with the process and execution.

_____

_____

_____

_____

_____

"By this all people
will know that you
are My disciples:
if you have love
for one another."

John 13:35

If you're a Christian entrepreneur, you have a great opportunity to shine the light of Christ to the world through your business and connections. Think about the connections you have right now as a result of owning and operating your own company. Who can you influence for the Gospel?

Our verse this week is very specific in detailing how people will know we belong to and follow Christ. It's about the love. Show some love, right! At work, we have so many avenues in which to show love. It's not only through person-to-person contact, but also through our presence online. What do we post? Can people tell we follow Christ by our words, actions, and posts?

What does this love look like? Well, it's not what; it's Who. The way we show love should look like Christ. Do we have kind responses and patience with others? Do we look out for the best interests of others more than our own? Does humility dominate our personality, or does pride?

Dear LORD,

Help me to show Your love to others. The people You bring into my life need to see more of You and less of me. Help me to extend love in the specific ways that are needed for each point of contact. Lord, give me loving words to speak. Help my actions to be loving. Help me to humble myself and give love even when I don't feel like it. Help me to love even when I don't think someone deserves it. You are the definition of love, Jesus. As a child of God, I want to reflect You to the lost and dying world I come into contact with every day. Give me strength and courage to do this through my business – whether I'm "clocked-in" or not.

AMEN

This week, think about how you can show love to others on the job. How can you extend love to your employees, customers, other business owners, and even your community? Our witness can go a long way to point others to Christ.

_____

_____

_____

_____

_____

REST

Are you ready for a break? Do you feel like you run and run and run and never get everything caught up? Have you been able to take a day off from your business or even possibly go on vacation and shut things down for a time? Do you feel guilty for resting from your work? Or do you find it hard to take time off because there's always something that must be done?

For the next 5 weeks, focus on rest. Think about the amount of rest you've been able to take while operating your business - or maybe the lack of rest. It's important that we take time periodically to step away from the day-to-day operations and refresh in our spirit, renew our body, and restore our strength and health. We were not made to go full force all day every day of the year.

"By the seventh
day God had
finished the work
He had been doing;
so on the seventh
day He rested from
all his work."

Genesis 2:2

This week, specifically, let's look at the example of rest that God has given us. If He thought rest was important, then we should too. He gives purpose to the rest we take. And He lets us know, by His own example, that rest does not equal laziness. It gives peace and helps us focus on our families and our relationship with the Lord. It is good to take a break. How long has it been since you have rested from your work?

God didn't rest because He was tired. He's God; He *"never sleeps or slumbers."* (Psalm 121:4)

He rested because His work was completed. Nothing more needed to be added. No more labor was required. He rested because He was pleased with all He had done. "It was good." He also rested to establish one of the basic rhythms of Creation. He set an example, a precedent, by showing us rest alongside hard work.

God set the requirement of rest at creation because He desires His people to live lives pleasing to Him, full of worship and adoration. We were never meant to "go" and "do" and "produce" all the time, every waking minute of our lives.

The world tries to tell us we need to work hard all the time and never take time off or else we will miss out on making more money. But we have several well-known businesses in our country who are notorious for being closed on Sundays. Newsflash: those businesses are still operating today and their profits are very good. They set an example to us that we shouldn't fear missing a sale, but instead should fear a holy God more.

Dear LORD,

Thank You for setting the example of rest for me. Thank You for showing me the value of rest and the benefit it has for my mind, body, and soul. Relieve me of any fears or anxieties I have when contemplating taking a time of rest from my work. Help me to detach from my business so it doesn't own me. I want to be surrendered to You and not mastered by my company. Help me to spend my time in rest focused on You and those You have placed in my life. As I take periods of rest, I pray You replenish my strength. I pray You restore my energy so I will be ready to work when I return to my labors. I pray You renew my mind and give me peace when I step away from my job. Refresh my spirit and give me a right heart and attitude so I can continue doing what I was called to do, and to do it well.

AMEN

We are commanded to "keep the Sabbath" – this carries the same idea of resting from all our labors and instead to honor God. By doing this, we show the Lord that we depend on Him for provision. We lean on His strength to give us all that's needed. So, have you taken time to cease from exertion in your business? Have you set aside time to be still from your labor? If not, will you consider incorporating a specific time in your company to abstain from work?

"I sought the Lord,
and He answered
me and rescued me
from all my fears."

Psalm 34:4

The first step is to seek the Lord. When we have fears and issues that plague our minds or seem out of our control, we need to go to the One who is able to provide the wisdom and discernment needed to solve the problem. We are told over and over in the Bible not to fear, but here we are told what to do when we fear.

We need to seek the Lord for guidance because He hears our prayers and He answers our calls for help. Our verse this week even goes so far as to say the Lord will rescue us from our fears. And not just some fears, but all our fears. We need that rescue. It is unproductive to continue in fear and it cripples our ability to devote our undivided attention to the tasks that need completed.

When we seek the Lord, and He answers us, everything else will fall into place. There is an order. Instead of trying to handle things on our own or seek ungodly help, we need to go to the One who has already gone before us. He already knows the outcome and He's just waiting for us to come to Him and ask for His help and intervention.

Let's set aside our fear and pride this week and reach out to the Lord, and call on Him to meet us in our place of weakness and vulnerability, and rescue us. He is near. He sees us. He hears us. And He already knows what's on our hearts.

Dear LORD,

Help me to always seek You first and to make You my first priority before seeking anything or anyone else. I want You to be my "go-to" before I seek the world. I pray that when I come to You, You will hear my prayers and answer me. I pray for intervention with the fears I have for my business. Those things I cannot control with my work, Lord, I pray You handle them for me. I pray You give me guidance and wisdom to know how to answer and where to find a solution. I pray You put godly influences and people in my path to help me when I encounter roadblocks in my job. Lord, above all, I pray You rescue me from my fears so they don't inhibit my progress and success as a business owner. Give me Your confidence and assurance as You walk beside me through each fear I have.

AMEN

What are you fearing this week? As business owners, there are always a host of things that can go wrong at any given moment. Most of them are beyond our control and sometimes we have to seek outside help to solve the issue. This could be technological problems, shipping or manufacturing problems, or it could simply be an unhappy customer and their bad experience. We need to be reminded what to do when these fears arise. And Psalm 34:4 tells us exactly that.

"Come to me, all of
you who are weary
and burdened, and I
will give you rest."

Matthew 11:28

God's Word addresses the approach we are to take with our activities. The first step: come to Christ. How do we come to Him? We pray – call on His Name and ask Him for rest. Take each concern and stress to Jesus that you have regarding your company. As you read His Word, the Bible, ask Him to speak to your heart regarding those burdens you've been carrying with your business. He understands.

As business owners, we carry a host of burdens. We can easily become weary from the day-to-day operations and interactions with employees and customers. It seems there is always something that has to be done, and the work is never finished. Once a project is completed, there is another that pops up in its place. Often, these new projects are brought on with the excitement of finding new ways to build revenue and reach customers with your products or services. But over time, it seems the project is a hindrance and takes more time than we are willing to spend toward its completion.

As we come to the Lord with our burdens and concerns, we need to seek His wisdom, guidance, and discernment as to how we are to lighten our load or make it easier for us to carry. He has already gone before us, so He is the perfect person to help us with this task. We were not meant to be heavily burdened with our work to the point of breaking. Jesus wants to give us rest. He wants us to be refreshed and re-energized in our work so we will serve Him with a renewed vibrance and joy.

He will give us rest. He will ease, and relieve, and refresh our souls. We just need to come to Him. Let's do that this week!

Dear LORD,

When I am overburdened with my work, remind me to come to You. When I am weary from all I have been doing and all that is still to be done, help me not to get overwhelmed; but instead, to retreat to You. Refresh me as I spend time in Your Word. Relieve me of my burdens as I come to You in prayer. Send me the help I need to satisfy the demands of my work. Protect my mind from the attacks of the enemy when I feel weary from my job and weighed down by the tasks that remain unfinished. I want to come to You as my first response. I need Your refreshment, Your wisdom, and Your guidance. I need Your discernment this week with the projects that lay before me. I need Your help in managing my calendar and schedule. I pray You remove things that don't need my attention. I want to please You, Lord, with my time, money, and resources. Help me to prioritize my tasks this week.

AMEN

Are you carrying burdens this week? Has it been a long year? Matthew 11:28 invites us to come to Christ and receive the rest we need from our burdens and weariness. He is the only One who can offer satisfying rest and refresh our minds, bodies, and souls.

"He gives strength to the weary, and to him who lacks might He increases power. Though youths grow weary and tired, and vigorous young men stumble badly, yet those who wait for the Lord will gain new strength; they will mount up with wings like eagles, they will run and not get tired, they will walk and not become weary."

Isaiah 40:29-31

There are often many demands placed on business owners, and it can be overwhelming at times. But as we trust in the Lord, we will find new strength. Strength that we didn't have previously. And it comes to us by waiting in the Lord. We can count on Him to lift us up, as our verse says. Our job is to hope in Him and His Word, abide in Him, and depend on Him each day.

This takes humility on our part, and a little bit of patience. More times than not, we want to take the wheel, and be in control, and run everything in our own strength. But it doesn't take long before we run into a wall and realize we are not strong enough to carry the load that has been placed on us. We need the shoulders of Christ to help us carry the tasks.

As we trust in Him, He will encourage us and give us strength to do the work we have to do. We just need to humble ourselves and ask for His help. He will relieve us of the weight and carry our load. This relief will give us new energy to walk, run, and fly through our days and weeks. And it all starts with seeking Him, trusting Him, and placing our hope in Him and His strength.

Dear LORD,

You give power to the weak and strength to the powerless. When I am weak and tired and fall in exhaustion, help me find new strength in You. When I worry about meeting deadlines, help me to trust in You to help me soar above my heavy load. Give me a second wind to complete the tasks before me. Provide the strength that is needed to run my company and make the decisions that are needed. Help me to have the energy to deal with customers and employees without getting weary or faint. Encourage me as I spend time in Your Word and prayer. And surround me with other like-minded, Christian entrepreneurs who will come alongside me when I feel alone. Thank You for Your strong arms to carry me through my workload week after week.

AMEN

As business owners, we need all the strength we can get. We need strength and energy to run our company and keep it running. We need strength to deal with employees and customers. We need strength to fill orders and keep inventory in stock. We need strength to keep our marketing and advertising going. And sometimes, all these tasks are too much for our own strength. We need the strength of Another. And Isaish 40:29-31 tells us exactly Who provides that strength!

_____

_____

"The steadfast
of mind You will
keep in perfect
peace, because
he trusts in You."

Isaiah 26:3

To be steadfast in mind means to brace, uphold, or support. In other words, those with minds fully braced, upheld, and supported by Truth and who trust in God – will be kept in perfect peace. The key is to have our minds fixed on God.

God will guard us and keep us in peace when our mind, inclination, and character remain fixed on Him. We need to commit ourselves to Him, leaning on Him at all times, and hoping confidently in Him.

God sees and knows things we don't. We need to trust Him with all aspects of our job, even when we don't understand. We need to focus on His Truth when circumstances are hard. We need to trust God to the point where we fully turn control of our life and our business over to Him. God is good at being God!

Dear Lord,

Help me to trust You and keep my mind focused on You. Help me to trust You with every decision I make in my company. Help me to trust You with the outcome. Give me peace as I commit myself to You and give You control. I pray You go before me and help me to remain by Your side, listening to Your guidance and obeying Your commands. Help me not to lean on the world, or the latest fads and schemes. I want to be fully braced, upheld, and supported by Your truth. So many things seek to steal my peace, but I want to trust in You so that I may rest each night knowing that You are taking care of me. When I am tempted to become distracted and overwhelmed by everything around me, bring my attention and focus back to You.

Amen

Where do your thoughts take you this week? What is your mind focused on? As entrepreneurs, there never seems to be a lack of things to think about regarding our businesses. Operating a company brings a lot of mental baggage, and sometimes this results in a lack of sleep. But as Isaiah 26:3 reminds us, we have One who will keep us in perfect peace as we focus our thoughts and minds on Him.

_____

_____

_____

BLESSING

What a year it has been!
There may have been some ups
and downs, but stay faithful in
prayer. We have been praying
for our businesses for the past
45 weeks and we are nearing
the end of one year of prayer.
The Lord hears our prayers
and He knows our hearts for
the work that we do. Remain
steadfast and finish strong
in the praying work you are
doing for your company!

As we finish out the
year of praying for our
businesses, these final 7 weeks
will focus on praying for
God's favor and blessings
over our companies.
We need the favor of the
Lord as He opens doors and
makes a way for us to shine
His light into the world.
And we need the refreshment
that comes from
receiving His blessings.

"May the favor
of the Lord our
God rest upon us;
establish the work
of our hands for us
– yes, establish the
work of our hands."

Psalm 90:17

We need the help, intervention, and favor of the Lord to make our efforts successful. When we have His favor, He is showing approval. He is making a way where there is no way. He is doing for us what we cannot do for ourselves. We need this help because we are not able to do it in our own strength.

Certainly there are things affecting our jobs right now that are out of our control or beyond our skill set. We need the wisdom and guidance of the Lord to show us how to navigate these seasons in our company. We need to rely on His discernment to direct us in the way we should go, and the things we should decline, and the changes that need to take place.

There will be varying levels of difficulty in the work that we do. There may be new skills to learn, or new help to hire, or new friends to be made in order to grow our business and be profitable in the world today. We need to be flexible, teachable, and humble with people and tasks. And we need to pray the Lord will protect us from the attacks of the enemy who lurks around every corner watching us and taking note of our weaknesses and reactions. We need to pray God will keep us safe and that we will keep our emotions in check.

We should not forget that many battles and situations in the Bible we read were victorious and had good outcomes because the favor of the Lord was on the people. We can put our hands to work on many different things, but we need the favor of the Lord on that work. Our work for Him is not in vain – it has purpose. Our work for the Lord has permanence in the lives of others when His hand of favor and blessing is on it.

Dear LORD,

I pray You give me favor in my work. Lord, bless the work of my hands in all I do. Go before me and make a way, open doors where You want me to be, and close doors where I should not enter. Protect my business, Lord, and help me to have wisdom and discernment with relationships and decisions that affect my company. I want Your approval more than my own or that of another. Help me to form connections in my community and with other entrepreneurs. Help me to grow my business and prosper in the work that I do. Thank You Lord for the many blessings You've already given me. I wouldn't be able to have the opportunities I have or to do what I do without Your blessings and assistance.

AMEN

This week specifically, let's pray for God's favor to establish the work of our hands. What work do your hands have left to do this week? Are there projects to finish up? Are there tasks left undone from last week? Are you making plans for the months ahead? Lift those up to the Lord and ask Him for favor with those tasks.

_____

_____

_____

_____

"And my God will
supply all your
needs according to
his riches in glory
in Christ Jesus."

Philippians 4:19

God is a good Father who provides for His children. He knows what we need. He sees where we are lacking. We may be tempted to feel vulnerable or insecure when our needs go unmet, but we must remember that security is found in Christ.

We have trouble wrapping our minds around the help God provides, because we try to relate in human terms. We meet others' needs according to our ability, but God meets needs according to His riches! He is not limited in the ways we are. We only have a finite amount of time, money, and resources. God's resources are infinite and unlimited.

God will liberally supply – meaning, fill to the fullest – your every need, according to His riches in glory in Christ Jesus. So don't be afraid to take your needs to Him. Go to Him in prayer and confess those needs that fill your mind. Let God know where You need His help in your business. Let Him know where You need provision, and ask Him to intervene. He is ready and willing to help.

Dear LORD,

You already know my needs. You see where I am lacking. You know my finances, and You know the expenses that wait for me in the future. Lord, I need Your help in providing for each need that arises in my company. I pray You step in and supply for me what is needed so that I may continue the work I have set out to do. Help me to rely on You, trust You, and wait for You. I don't want to try and run ahead of You. I also don't want to seek other means of supplying my needs and forsake You. Fill me with hope and assurance that my needs will be met. And help me to use the blessings You give me to be a blessing for others. I don't want to hoard my blessings. I want to turn around and help someone else. I want Your blessings to flow through me and my business to those around me – customers, staff, and vendors.

AMEN

What are the needs of your company this week? What are the needs that remain this year? Do you need funding? Do you need new product ideas? Do you need a new way to advertise your services? Do you need a better way to correspond with your customers? Do you need to upgrade your technology? As a business owner, it seems the list of needs are always growing. But Philippians 4:19 gives us good reason to not despair.

"Give, and it will be given to you; a good measure-pressed down, shaken together, and running over-will be poured into your lap. For with the measure you use, it be measured back to you."

Psalm 90:17

When we think about God's favor and blessings, we normally think about how we can receive them. We may not always think about how we can be a blessing to others or give favor to someone else. But our verse this week reminds us that it comes full circle how we treat others and the way we are treated and receive back. There is a direct correlation between the two. And it's important that we acknowledge the connection.

It all begins with giving. "Give" is the first word of our verse this week. It's important that we don't get hung up on receiving. We need to establish the act of giving, and do it regularly.

We are told, "Give and you will receive." By giving, we are opening doors of friendship and establishing relationships with others. We are connecting with them in a way that meets a need. And when the time comes for our needs to be met, they will remember our kindness and come to our aid.

It's not that we just "receive." Our verse tells us our gift will return to us in full! And the process of this fullness is further explained and described. There is a pressing down and shaking together that is taking place. Just like filling a trash can, and you press the trash down so you can fit more in. Or you tap a container on the counter to try and settle the contents so you have room to add more.

And not just that it's more, but our verse says it's so much that it runs over and pours into your lap! Wow! That's quite the return! What other investment rewards you in that way? Where in your business can you give back? Where in your community can your company get involved to give back? What about with your customers who have been loyal to you? Is there a need that you can meet?

What you give determines what you get back. This goes with effort, with money, with kindness, with time, etc. The measure you use when you bless others, will be used to measure back to you. As you extend kindness, then kindness will be returned to you; and so on.

Dear LORD,

I pray You open my eyes to the ways I can give of my company's products to help others. Show me how I can offer the services of my company to be of use to someone. Give me wisdom and discernment each time an opportunity arises to give a donation or offer help. Help me not to have a prideful heart or be jaded toward giving. Help me to be moved with compassion for others and to extend kindness in their time of need. Help me not to be stingy with what I give but to give openly, freely, and with a genuine and cheerful heart. Help me to want to help and give, and to do so willingly. I don't want to give out of obligation, ever. Help me be attentive to the ways in which I can give toward my staff, my customers, and my community. Help me not to give just because I think or expect that I will be returned a favor, or that it will make me or my company look good. I pray each act of giving I do will bring honor and glory to Your Name.

AMEN

Pray this week and ask the Lord to show you areas where you can give. Ask Him to help you see how to give, because maybe it's not always money that is helpful, but rather time, or a kind gesture. Maybe you can donate your items to a local shelter. Maybe you can donate your services to single moms or widows or disabled people. Ask the Lord to give you wisdom and guidance as you consider giving of yourself and your company.

_____

_____

_____

_____

_____

_____

_____

_____

_____

_____

_____

"Protect me,
God, for I take
refuge in You."

Psalm 16:1

This verse reminds us that we need to call on One higher than ourselves to keep us safe. We can only do what is humanly possible to protect our company, but God is infinitely higher and more powerful than we are. We need His help above all. As He protects us, He preserves us; and we need His intervention to preserve our company.

This verse also reminds us that there will be times when we are overwhelmed and weary from the continual operations of our business and we need to come to the Lord for refuge. That phrase, "take refuge in," means to confide in, take hope in, or put trust in. We need to confide in the Lord and hope in Him. He is worthy of our trust and He is the only One who already knows what we need.

What do we need protection from as business owners? Everything! We need protection for the physical building of our company. Or if it's online – we need cyber security, right? There are so many ways for people to break in and cause harm, whether physically or technologically through our website, social media accounts, company computer systems, as well as banking and finances.

We need protection of our finances and company assets, and this comes by wisdom and discernment of the business decisions we make. It is also important that we protect ourselves from bad alliances or bad influences on our company. There are many ways we can be ill-advised, so we need to stay vigilant and have wisdom when seeking guidance and counsel for our business.

It's not just us, personally, or even the company itself – but also the employees who need protection. We need to be seeking the Lord for the protection and safety of those who work for us, as well as those customers who utilize our services and purchase our products. And ultimately, we need to be praying for protection from the attacks of the evil one. The enemy seeks to take us under, and he will use any means necessary to smear our name and give our company a bad reputation. We need protection from any and all attacks he tries to launch our way – whether legally through lawsuits or verbally through bad reviews and bad press.

Dear Lord,

I pray for the protection of my company. Not only for the things included in the day-to-day operations, but also for me, personally. I pray for protection from the physical, mental, and spiritual attacks of the enemy that try to knock me down and prevent progress in my business. I pray that I will always confide in You, Lord, for relief from the heat of life. I want to continually trust in You for protection and for reprieve from the burdens that come with running my own business. Lord, You've already gone before me and You know what's up ahead in the life of my company. I pray for protection from anything that seeks to disrupt Your good plans for me and my business. I pray I continually set my hope in You as You cover me and keep me safe.

Amen

Where do you go for relief from the heat of life? When the sun is beating down on you, you seek shade. But when you're in the thick of it with your work, where do you go or what do you do to find "shade"? This week, when you are feeling the heat of the world coming down on you as you run your business, let Psalm 16:1 challenge you to seek God for shelter.

_____

_____

_____

_____

_____

_____

_____

_____

_____

_____

_____

"May the Lord bless
you and protect you;
may the Lord make His
face shine on you and
be gracious to you;
may the Lord look
with favor on you and
give you peace."

Numbers 6:24-26

Our verses this week are some of the more familiar verses we think to associate with God's favor. When we seek God's favor, we are seeking His support, approval, and kindness. Ultimately, we are seeking His blessing.

As Christian entrepreneurs, we not only desire His protection over our lives, but also our businesses. We want Him to keep watch over us and guard us from evil. But we also desire God's blessing. We want His loving kindness to flow through every area of our lives.

These verses also encourage us to not only seek His blessing and protection, but also His mercy and grace. We need Him to go before us open doors we cannot open and close doors where we need not enter. We need Him to do for us what we cannot do for ourselves. We need His intervention in our business decisions.

We also need Him to enlighten us with understanding as we operate our businesses. And as He gives us greater knowledge about business, management, marketing, technology, and other areas of our work, He also gives us peace of mind and heart. He lifts us up with His approving countenance, giving us confident assurance that He is with us and all is well.

Dear LORD,

I pray for Your blessings on my company, my workers, my customers, and my suppliers. I pray Your favor on my life as I work each day and each week. I pray You will cover me and keep watch so the enemy does not succeed in his attempts to steal, kill, and destroy. I pray for Your grace and mercy to intervene in my workplace and provide in supernatural ways. I ask that You give me greater understanding in areas of weakness, and where I have much room for growth. I humbly ask for Your favor, Lord, and that You will give me Your peace so that I may sleep each night, knowing You are supporting me. I pray Your loving kindness continues forever.

AMEN

Where do you need God's favor in your business? Where do you need His strong arms of protection to cover your company? In what areas do you need His peace?

_____

_____

_____

_____

_____

"He who dwells in the shelter of the Most High will abide in the shadow of the Almighty. I will say to the Lord, "My refuge and my fortress, my God, in whom I trust."

Psalm 91:1-2

As the year winds down and comes to a close, maybe you are in need of some much-needed rest. It's been a busy year. It's been a wild and crazy year. But this year may have also included dry and slow seasons. The roller coaster of ups and downs in our companies adds stress and exhaustion to our bodies, and we need rest. Our verse this week tells us where to go for that rest and Who gives that rest.

When the rain and storms of our work are coming down, we need to find shelter. God provides that shelter for us. Our verse says we are to "dwell" in His shelter. We need to live in it, abide in it, make it our home, and be settled in the shelter of God – the place of protection He provides.

As we remain in Him, He helps us remain stable and fixed – at peace despite our surroundings or circumstances. He provides this peace for us because we choose to lean on His wisdom, rely on His understanding, and trust in His plans and purposes for our life and the life of our company. He is the object of our peace. He is the object of our hope. And He is the object of our trust. There is no one and nothing higher than our Most High God.

Dear LORD,

I pray for the rest that only You can provide. You know the schedule I've been keeping each week and each month. You see the exhaustion and stress that is involved. You know the struggles that are encountered and the directions things have gone for my company. I pray for relief from my job. I pray for a break and a season of rest to sit in Your shade and dwell in Your shelter. Refresh me during this time of rest. Renew my energy and spirit so I can return to work restored and ready to do what You have called me to do. I pray as You provide this time of rest, that I will surrender to it and not be tempted to pick up side projects or be distracted with other tasks. I don't want to be cheated out of the rest You provide. I want to receive the full benefit. Thank You for being my refuge and my fortress. I trust You Lord.

AMEN

He alone is our refuge, our place of safety; therefore, we should go to Him for rest, relief, and reprieve from the busy-ness of our work and our hectic schedules. He knows just what we need and when we need it. So abide in Him, and rest in His provision.

_____

_____

_____

_____

"For I know the
plans I have for you:
– this is the Lord's
declaration- Plans
for your well-being,
not for disaster, to
give you a future
and a hope."

Jeremiah 29:11

We have come to the end of our year of praying over our businesses! Congratulations for finishing strong and seeing it through! This final week of prayer is focused on the future. I don't know of a better verse for this other than Jeremiah 29:11. It's important that you remember: God has plans for you and He has plans for your business. He wants to give you a future and a hope. Now that's a great way to end one year and anticipate the things to come in the New Year!

God has plans for our lives and in order for us to see those plans come to fruition, we need God's direction, and we need to surrender to His ruling in our lives. We need to humbly obey all He is calling us to do. Sometimes God's plans don't unfold immediately. His timing is not always our timing. And His ways are not always our ways. But our job is to trust Him while we wait for His plans to develop and manifest in our lives.

We may have some big plans for our company in the New Year, but God's plans are greater. We may be planning new products, new services, new ways of reaching our customers, or perhaps expanding our business in other areas – or even locations! Our plans are obviously good, in our minds. We are thinking about our success and growth as business owners. But our verse says God's plans for us area also good, and we are given details as to how good His plans are.

God plans for our well-being – and this includes His thoughts. He thinks about us all the time. No one thinks more about us or our businesses more than the Lord. His thoughts toward us are for peace and not for evil. That's why we can trust Him and His plans. He wants to give us hope in our final outcome.

Many people can promise a host of things to us or for our companies, but God is the only One who can follow through on His promises every time. All of God's promises are yes and amen! So whatever plans you have made for this coming year, take them to the Lord and ask for His help so your plans can align with God's. He has already gone before us. He already knows the challenges we will face next year. He knows the ways to bring success in our businesses next year. He knows what will work and what will be in vain.

We need to seek His plans above our own so He can show us how to steward our companies for Him and bring honor and glory to His Name. We need His wisdom and discernment to guide us in the New Year. We need His favor and blessing on us as we seek to continue doing all He has called us to. We need His protection and provision because there will be things in the New Year that are beyond our control and that we will not be able to do in our own strength.

Dear LORD,

Thank You for allowing me to operate my business this past year. Thank You for giving me the talents, skills, and resources to be able to serve my customers. Thank You for being with me each step of the way - through every valley, and up each mountain. Go with me in this New Year, Lord, and show me the plans You have for me and my company. Open my eyes to see Your hand on my life. Open my ears and give me understanding as You show me the plans You have for me. Give me an open heart to receive Your plans, and a willingness to obey You in whatever You ask me to do and wherever You tell me to go. My business belongs to You, Lord. I am only a steward of what You have entrusted to me. Help me to steward my company well in this new year.

AMEN

Take some time this week and thank God for the year you have been able to endure. Thank Him for the year of opportunities He allowed you to have. Thank Him for giving you the skills and talents and resources to operate your company. And then spend time in prayer asking Him to reveal His plans to you. Ask Him to show you the plans He has for you and your business in this new year. We serve a great God. He is a mighty Father. And He is worthy of all praise!

_____

_____

_____

_____

_____

_____

_____

_____

_____

_____

_____

Let us introduce ourselves!

Hello! We are Janis and Shelby, the mother/daughter duo working together to form Real Live Faith.

At a time when both of us were searching and restless for the next step, we began asking God what He would have us do. We prayed and asked Him to reveal His plan for us. We had been contemplating the idea of starting a website for about three years, but didn't quite know how to progress with it. The Lord had been showing us little by little what His plan for us was, but it wasn't until we put our heads together and really sat down and put some time into our decision, that we said, "maybe He wants us to go into business together". That was a scary thought, but once we started this journey, there was no going back. We took that step of obedience, answering the call of God on our lives, and He has abundantly blessed the development and growth of Real Live Faith ever since. He knit together the details in ways we didn't even realize we needed, and continues to send us confirmation that we are right where He wants us to be.

It is our prayer that together we can *"draw near with confidence to the throne of grace, that we may receive mercy and may find grace to help in time of need"* (Hebrews 4:16). We don't know in what season of life you find yourself currently, but let this be a season of new life and growth. Wherever you are, whatever you are going through, remember that you are not alone in this world.

We would love to encourage you in your journey to discover and live out Real. Live. Faith!

For His Glory,
Janis & Shelby

Did you know we have a blog and podcast too?

We publish new blog posts and podcast episodes every other
week! The Real Live Faith Podcast is available to stream on
Apple Podcasts, Spotify, Amazon Music, and more.
Email subscribers receive early access to podcast episodes,
and other special perks!

Visit *reallivefaith.com* to sign up for our emails
and receive an exclusive, new-subscriber freebie!

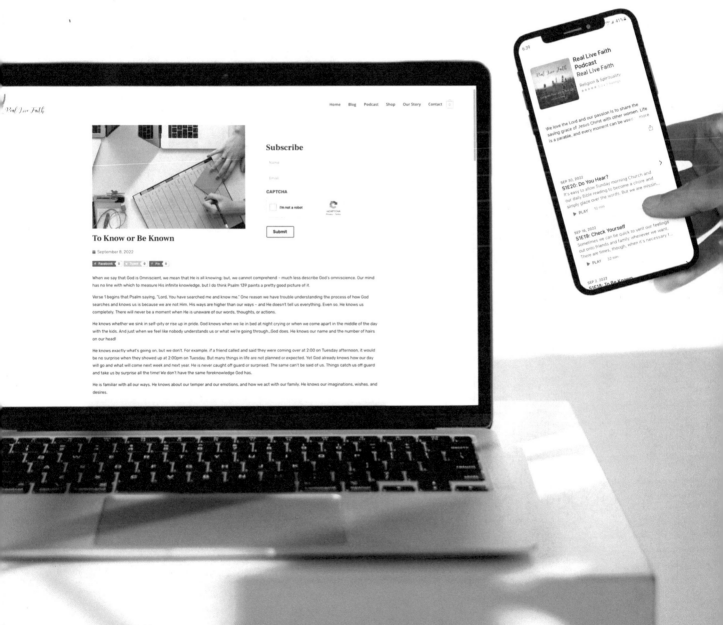

A Year of Thanks is a journal designed to help you foster
an attitude of gratitude. Both the Floral Edition and Rustic
Edition include beautifully designed artwork and photos for
each month of the year, and contain corresponding pages
to record things you're thankful for every day!

Visit *reallivefaith.com/shop* to see our printed
and digital PDF Gratitude Journals available!

Advent is a five week Christmas devotional outlining the origin and purpose of the Advent season. In this devotinal, you will find a focus verse and challenge question to go along with each week's theme, leading up to Christmas day. It's amazing how just five weeks of meditating on the reason for the season can challenge and grow your faith!

Visit *reallivefaith.com/shop* to see more devotionals available!

Made in the USA
Columbia, SC
21 December 2024